TRUE OR FALSE?

These are the bones from two human feet.

EVIDENCE EVIDENCE EVIDENCE EVIDENCE EVIDENCE EVIDENCE EVIDENCE

FALSE!

The foot below is human. The one to the left is the hind paw of a bear.

It's the job of a forensic anthropologist to tell the difference. Say a bone is found in the woods. The first question a forensic anthropologist has to answer is: Did this come from a human or an animal?

Here's one way she can tell. Look again at the feet. The bear foot has a narrower, longer heel bone than the human foot.

What else can forensic anthropologists figure out? Keep reading.

Book design Red Herring Design/NYC

Library of Congress Cataloging-in-Publication Data
Denega, Danielle.
Skulls and skeletons : true-life stories of bone detectives / by
Danielle Denega.
p. cm. — (24/7 : science behind the scenes)
Includes bibliographical references and index.
ISBN-13: 978-0-531-26200-9 (lib. bdg.)   978-0-531-26225-2 (pbk.)
ISBN-10: 0-531-26200-6 (lib. bdg.)   0-531-26225-1 (pbk.)
1. Forensic anthropologists. 2. Forensic anthropology. I. Title.
GN69.8.D46 2007
614'.17—dc22   2006021229

SKULLS AND SKELETONS

True-life Stories of Bone Detectives

Danielle Denega

WARNING: All of the cases in this book are true. They all involve dead bodies—and bones. Sometimes, only pieces of bones remain. These bones reveal the secrets of the dead.

Franklin Watts®
A Division of Scholastic Inc.
New York • Toronto • London • Auckland • Sydney
Mexico City • New Delhi • Hong Kong
Danbury, Connecticut

3

CONTENTS

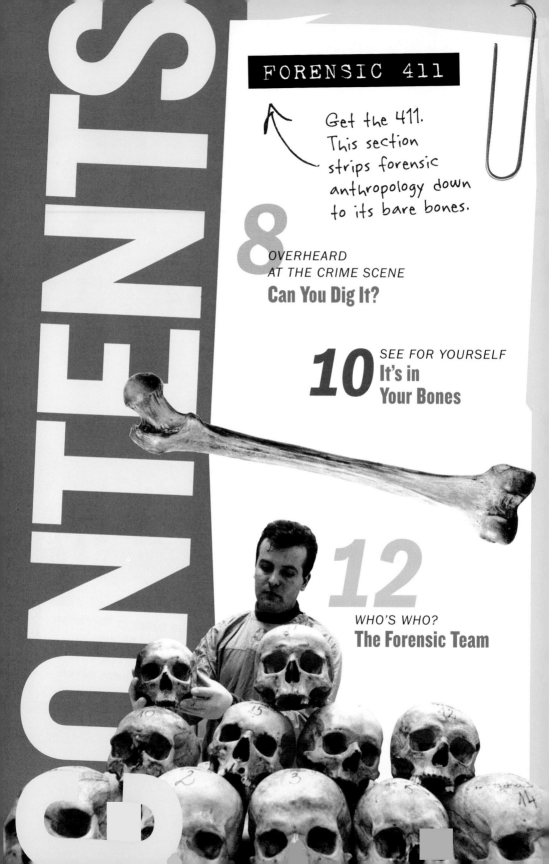

Find out how forensic anthropologists dug up some answers to these real mysteries.

In 1993, corpses in Hardin, MO, are buried for the second time.

15 Case #1:
The Hardin Cemetery Flood
After a huge flood, hundreds of bodies in a cemetery float to the surface. Can forensic anthropologists help ID the dead?

25 Case #2:
Murder in Guatemala
Two journalists are murdered in Guatemala. Can forensic anthropologists locate and identify their remains?

Bone remains are bagged in Guatemala.

In Thailand, anthropologists examine ancient skeletons.

35 Case #3:
The Princess of Khok Phanom Di
An anthropologist uncovers gravesites that date back more than 4,000 years. What secrets will the skeletons reveal?

5

FORENSIC DOWNLOAD

Here's even more amazing stuff about forensic anthropology for you to dig into.

YELLOW PAGES

FORENSIC 411

There's been a murder. Or a plane crash. Or a natural disaster. Only the bones of the victims remain.
Investigators want to know: Whom did the bones belong to? Was the victim male or female? Young or old? Tall or short? How did he or she die? Forensic anthropologists have the answers.

IN THIS SECTION:

▶ how to talk like a FORENSIC ANTHROPOLOGIST;

▶ how BONES reveal their secrets;

▶ whom anthropologists work with to identify bodies after CRIMES OR DISASTERS.

Can You Dig It?

Forensic anthropologists have their own way of speaking. Find out what their vocabulary means.

skeleton
(SKEL-uh-tuhn) the bony framework of the body

"Let's try to **excavate** the grave as carefully as we can. We don't want to disturb the **remains**."

"If we're lucky, there will be more than just a **skeleton** left."

excavate
(EK-skuh-vate) to dig up and remove something

remains
(rih-MAYNZ) the leftover parts of a dead body

"Anthro" has to do with human beings. "Ology" means "the study of."

anthropology
(an-thruh-POL-uh-jee) the study of human beings, including their bones, language, and culture. Forensic anthropologists use their knowledge of bones to find the identity of people killed in accidents, disasters, crimes, and war.

An expert examines skulls from the 1995 massacre in Srebrenica, in the Republic of Bosnia and Herzegovina.

"All we have are bones. We'd better get someone who knows a lot about **anthropology**."

Say What?

Here's some other lingo a forensic anthropologist might use on the job.

"This guy is going to be tough to **identify**. There's not much of him left."

identify
(eye-DEN-tuh-fye) to establish who a person is

"Five people were reported missing in the last month. Get the **antemortem** medical records for each of them."

antemortem
(an-tee-MORE-tuhm) before death

"Ante" means "before." "Mortem" means "death."

"Let's do a **postmortem** exam on these remains. Maybe we'll get a match with one of the antemortems."

postmortem
(pohst-MORE-tuhm) after death

"Post" means "after."

DMORT
(DEE-mort) a team of experts who help identify victims and prepare them for burial after big disasters or accidents. It's short for *Disaster Mortuary Operational Response Team*.
*"Call **DMORT**. There are too many victims for us to handle."*

PMI
(PEE-em-eye) the time between when a person dies and when the body is discovered. It's short for *postmortem interval*.
*"This corpse has been in the woods a long time. I'd guess the **PMI** is at least two months."*

siding
(SYE-ding) the process of figuring out if a bone is from the left or right side of the body
*"We need to do a **siding** on the thigh bone. Is it from the right or left leg?"*

sutures
(SOO-churz) cracks that separate bones in the skull. Sutures close up as a person ages.
*"This is no adult. The **sutures** have not yet closed in the skull."*

GENDER: Male jaws tend to be square. Female jaws are more pointed.

RACE: Anthropologists can get clues about a person's race from:
▶ the length of the jaw
▶ the distance between the eyes
▶ the openings in the nose
▶ the slant of the cheekbones

HUMAN OR ANIMAL: Are the back teeth dull and the front teeth sharper? If so, they belonged to a human, not an animal.

male

female

AGE: Small children have baby teeth. Older children have permanent teeth. In older adults the teeth may be worn down.

OCCUPATION: When muscles get heavy use, bony ridges form where the muscle attaches to the bone. People who worked with their hands might have bony ridges on the bones of their wrists.

GENDER: Males tend to have narrower pelvic bones than females. A female pelvis is wider to allow for childbirth.

AGE: If the front of the pelvic bones are bumped or ridged, the person was young. Older people have smoother pelvic bones.

AGE: Teenagers have femurs, or thighbones, that are knobby.

AGE: Older adults may have signs of arthritis at the joints.

It's in Your Bones

How do forensic anthropologists get information from a pile of bones?

Consider this case: Two hikers find a pile of bones in the woods. Police think the bones belong to a person who was reported missing several months earlier. They need to know for sure. That's a typical case for a forensic anthropologist. How would she try to solve it? Here's a step-by-step guide:

1. Clean the bones. Use flesh-eating beetles to remove any flesh on the bones. If there's a rush, boil the bones in soapy water instead.

2. Decide if the bones are human. Anthropologists can tell the difference between human and animal bones.

3. Identify the bones. Decide which bones come from which part of the body. Then "side" the bones—figure out which side of the body they come from. Finally, lay the bones out the way they would appear in the body.

4. Examine the bones. Measure, weigh, and **x-ray** the bones. Study them under a **microscope**.

5. Create a postmortem profile. Create a description of the **victim**. Just a few bones can often reveal a victim's age, height, race, and **gender**. They can also reveal how long the victim has been dead and what may have caused the death.

6. Compare the profile to the antemortem records. Look at the missing person's medical records. Do the details match the postmortem profile?

Check out the skeletons on the opposite page. Find out how bones speak to an anthropologist.

The Forensic Team

When there's a big case, forensic anthropologists work with other experts. Here's a look at the team.

FORENSIC ANTHROPOLOGISTS
They're called in to identify victims by studying bones.

FORENSIC DNA SPECIALISTS
They collect DNA from blood or body fluids left at the scene. Then they use this evidence to identify victims and suspects.

FORENSIC PATHOLOGISTS
They figure out what diseases someone may have had.

FORENSIC DENTISTS
They identify victims and criminals by their teeth or bitemarks.

MEDICAL EXAMINERS
They're medical doctors who investigate suspicious deaths. They try to find out when and how someone died. They often direct other team members.

FINGERPRINT EXAMINERS
They find, photograph, and collect fingerprints at the scene. Then they compare them to prints they have on record.

CRIMINALISTS
They sketch or photograph the scene. They also look for and collect evidence—such as blood, hair, paint, glass, fibers, weapons, and tire marks.

POLICE DETECTIVES/ AGENTS
They are often the ones to collect evidence, investigate crimes, and arrest suspects.

FORENSIC TOXICOLOGISTS
They're called in to test victims for drugs, alcohol, and/or poison.

TRUE-LIFE CASE FILES!

24 hours a day, 7 days a week, 365 days a year, forensic anthropologists are solving mysteries.

IN THIS SECTION:

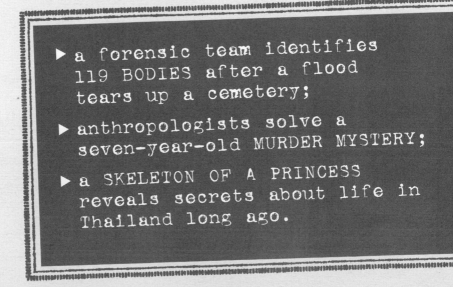

▶ a forensic team identifies 119 BODIES after a flood tears up a cemetery;

▶ anthropologists solve a seven-year-old MURDER MYSTERY;

▶ a SKELETON OF A PRINCESS reveals secrets about life in Thailand long ago.

Here's how forensic anthropologists get the job done.

What does it take to solve a crime? Good forensic anthropologists don't just make guesses. They're scientists. They follow a step-by-step process.

As you read the case studies, keep an eye out for the icons below. They'll clue you in to each step along the way.

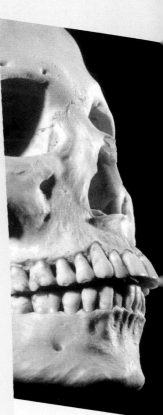

 THE QUESTION At the beginning of a case, forensic anthropologists identify **one or two main questions** they have to answer.

THE EVIDENCE The next step is to **gather and analyze evidence**. Forensic anthropologists collect as much information as they can. Then they study it to figure out what it means.

THE CONCLUSION Along the way, forensic anthropologists come up with theories to explain what may have happened. They test these theories against the evidence. Does the evidence back up the theory? If so, **they've reached a conclusion**. And chances are they've cracked the case!

Hardin, Missouri
July 1993

The Hardin Cemetery Flood

After a huge flood, hundreds of bodies in a small-town cemetery float to the surface. Can forensic anthropologists help identify the dead?

Water, Water Everywhere

Heavy rains bring terrible flooding to the Midwest.

Highway 40 in Missouri was completely underwater when the Missouri River flooded in 1993. Here, a rescue worker checks in over a walkie-talkie.

In the spring of 1993, it seemed like the rain would never end. Rivers overflowed their banks all across the Midwest. Flood waters ruined homes and businesses. Roads and bridges were washed away.

The flooding didn't end until the fall. By then, 534 counties in nine Midwestern states had been hit hard. Water covered more than 20 million acres (8 million hectares).

The results were terrible. Fifty people died, and 55,000 homes were damaged or destroyed. The flood caused more than $15 billion in damage. Much of the Midwest was declared a disaster area.

The event became known as the Great Flood of 1993. It was one of the worst natural disasters in American history.

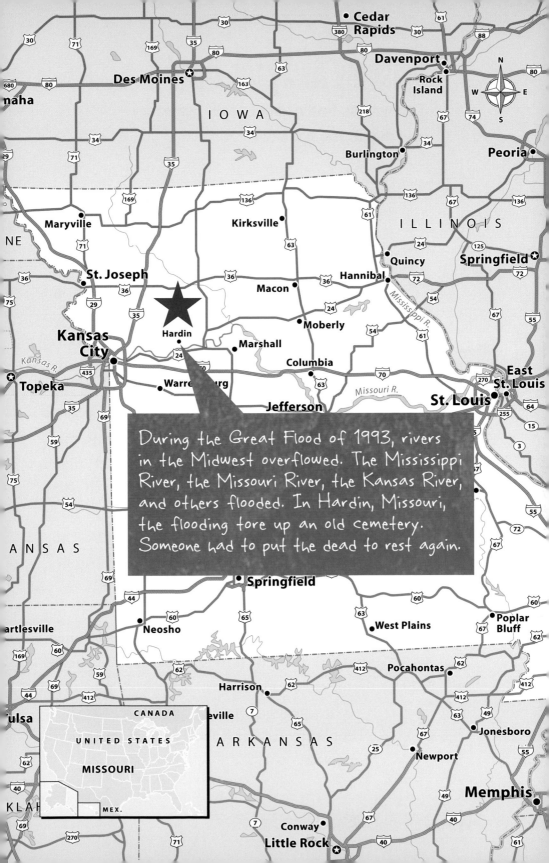

During the Great Flood of 1993, rivers in the Midwest overflowed. The Mississippi River, the Missouri River, the Kansas River, and others flooded. In Hardin, Missouri, the flooding tore up an old cemetery. Someone had to put the dead to rest again.

Washing Away the Dead

**The waters find a small-town cemetery—
and dig up the past.**

In July 1993, the floodwaters reached Hardin, Missouri. Hardin is a small farming town that lies six miles (10 km) north of the Missouri River. Only about 600 people lived there.

When the Missouri River flooded, the cemetery in Hardin was washed out. Coffins and human remains floated through streets and fields.

In Hardin, the flood not only destroyed homes and other buildings. The waters began to dig up the dead.

Hardin Cemetery was built in 1828. Nearly everyone in the tiny town buried their dead there. The **cemetery** sat in a low area. So when the flood hit, water rushed over the graves. It swept away hundreds of headstones, vaults, and caskets.

Nearly half of the 1,756 graves in Hardin Cemetery were destroyed. Coffins and human remains floated through streets and fields. Some ended up as far as 18 miles (29 km) away.

The people of Hardin were crushed. "People are just heartsick," one resident said to a reporter.

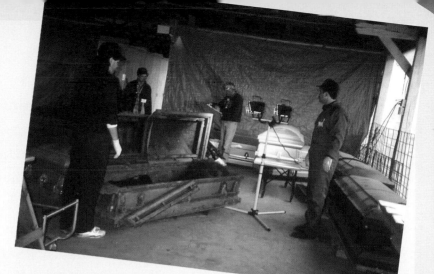

Search and Recovery

A team of forensic experts arrives to help recover the remains from Hardin Cemetery.

Anthropologists prepare to remove bones and remains from coffins found after the Hardin Cemetery flood.

Dean Snow is the county **coroner** in Hardin, Missouri. The people of Hardin wanted Snow to find and identify the remains.

Snow organized a special team. It included **forensic anthropologists** and **forensic pathologists** from DMORT. That's a team of **experts** put together by the federal government.

The team members' mission was clear. Could they find and identify the remains from the cemetery?

The first step was to search for these remains. Volunteers from the town helped.

The team eventually found nearly 600 caskets. Most of them had broken open. The bones had been scattered. In all, the volunteers recovered 3,400 bones, including 129 **crania**, or **skulls**.

DMORT stands for Disaster Mortuary Operational Response Team.

They stored the remains at the county fairgrounds in barns and refrigerated trucks. Next, the team created antemortem profiles of the missing dead. They looked for anything unusual about each person that would help identify his or her remains.

The team found 129 crania—skulls—from the Hardin Cemetery. Forensic anthropologists then sorted them by gender.

Forensic anthropologist Paul Sledzik worked on the project. Normally, profiles include medical and dental records. "But in the Hardin disaster," Sledzik said, "many of the missing had been dead for a very long time. Dental and medical records weren't always available."

To fill in the gaps, investigators talked to family members of the missing people. They set up an office at the fairgrounds. In the weeks after the flood, people came in to answer questions about their relatives. How did they die? Did they have any broken bones or diseases? What color were their coffins? What clothes were they buried in?

The answers helped create profiles for most of the people who had been buried in the cemetery.

Profiling the Missing Dead

Anthropologists begin sorting and analyzing the remains.

Now it was time to examine the bones. Paul Sledzik worked with three other forensic anthropologists on the postmortem exams.

The remains were in all states of **decomposition**, or decay. Some were new and well-preserved. Some were dried up like mummies. Some were skeletons. Others were just pieces of bones. A forensic pathologist handled the bodies that had a lot of soft **tissue** left. The anthropology team handled the remains that were mostly bones.

Some cases looked promising. Thirty-five of the caskets had complete skeletons inside. The anthropologists were able to measure the skulls and the **long bones**. They often found personal items inside the caskets. Some people had been buried with watches or blankets. The postmortem profiles for these people contained a lot of detail.

Some bodies had been torn from their coffins. So Slezdik and the others did what they could to create a profile. They measured bones to discover a person's age, race, and size. Sometimes the gender was obvious from outside organs left on the bodies. The anthropologists also looked for **evidence** of broken bones or disease.

Long bones have a long shaft and knobs on the two ends.

An anthropologist examines some remains found after the flood.

[Forensic Fact]
The longest bone in the human body is the thigh bone, which is called the femur. The length of your femur is about 1/4 of your height.

21

Anthropologists examine pelvic bones and sort them by gender.

The tibia is in your shin bone.

The femur is in your thigh.

And those were the easy cases. Most of the remains weren't bodies at all. The searchers had brought back thousands of bones. Sledzik and his team had lots of leg bones, arm bones, **pelvic** bones, and skulls. They had no idea which bones belonged together.

All of the bits and pieces had to be sorted. The anthropologists separated them by type. They put skulls in one place, **tibia** in another, **femurs** in another, and so on. Then, they tried to side the bones. Next, they grouped the bones according to age: infant, child, young adult, or older adult. Finally, they tried to separate males from females.

The team found it nearly impossible to put together whole skeletons. They did estimate the number of people whose remains they found. The flood had washed away the remains of 769 people. Almost 600 of them had been recovered.

Bones were sorted by size and side to determine how many people's remains were present.

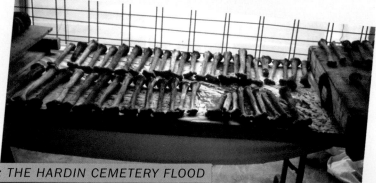

Putting the Dead to Rest

The dead are buried once again.

As the team finished examining the remains, they moved on to their final task. They compared the postmortem profiles to the antemortem profiles. Slowly, they began to identify bodies.

A monument was built at Hardin Cemetery to remember the dead who were washed away by the flood.

Some cases were easy to solve. A well-preserved body might be identified by a tattoo. A casket could be linked to a name by a piece of jewelry found inside.

In the end, Sledzik and the rest of the team identified the remains of 119 people.

By October 1993, the DMORT team had left town. The people of Hardin prepared to rebury the remains that could not be identified. Bones and pieces of bones were placed in 476 separate vaults. Each vault was carefully tagged so it could be linked with its postmortem profile.

Vernie Fountain led a team of funeral directors who helped in the disaster. He told the *New York Times* that the flood had been terrible for the families of the missing dead. "You bury someone and you expect them to be buried [forever]," he said. **24/7**

[Forensic Fact]
In 1994, the state of Missouri passed a law that was inspired by the Hardin flood disaster. It requires an ID tag to be placed in caskets with bodies and in urns containing cremated remains.

Paul Sledzik speaks about the role of anthropologists in mass disasters.

24/7: How is forensic anthroplogy useful in large disasters?

SLEDZIK: First, forensic anthrologists identify remains. Second, they help with the search and recovery. Third, they help manage the overall identification efforts.

24/7: How do mass disasters differ?

SLEDZIK: Are you dealing with whole bodies or parts of bodies? Are the bodies spread over a large area or in a small site? Is it a closed population disaster? (Plane crashes are a closed population disaster because you know how many people were on the plane.) Or is it an open population disaster—and you don't know how many people were involved?

24/7: Are there other challenges?

SLEDZIK: Sure. We have to get antemortem information to make an identification. In cases like Hurricane Katrina, records were flooded. So the information wasn't available.

24/7: Is it hard to work with family members of the victims?

SLEDZIK: Loved ones have to provide us with a lot of information. We, in turn, need to keep them informed about what's going on.

There was no crime committed in Hardin—just a disaster caused by nature. But in the next case, anthropologists try to solve a double murder.

Guatemala
Central America
1985

Murder in Guatemala

**Two American journalists are murdered
in Guatemala. Can forensic anthropologists
locate and identify their remains?**

From the 1950s to the 1990s, Guatemalans fought a brutal civil war. A rebel army hid out in the country's mountains. In 1985, two journalists from the U.S. went into those mountains to interview a rebel fighter. They never returned.

MEXICO

GUATEMALA

BELIZE

Trinitaria

Xultún

Tikal
Tikal

Nakum
Yaxjá

Belmop

Melchor de Mencos

Lago Petén

ores

Sayaxché
El Ceibal

Poptún

Gulf
Hond

Bahia de Amatique

Livingston
Rio Dulce

Puerto
Barrios

GUATEMALA

Todos Santos
Cuchumatán

CA 1

Zaculeu

Huehuetenango

Cobán

Languín

El Estor

Lago
de Izabal

Mariscos

Quiriguá   Quiriguá

San
Marcos

El Llano
village

Santa Cruz
del Quiché

Chichicastenango

Salamá

El
Progreso

Zacapa

Quetzaltenango

Totonicapán

Iximché

Chiquimula

Copán
Ruins

Santa
de Co

Ciudad
Tecún
Umán

Las Majadas
village

Solola

Lago de
Atitlán

Panajachel

Chimaltenango

Guatemala
City

Jalapa

HONDURAS

Retalhuleu

Mazatenango

Antigua
Guatemala

Lago de
Amatitlán

Nueva Ocotepeque

CA 2

Escuintla

CA 1

Tulate

Cuilapa

Jutiapa

Puerto
San José

Monterrico

Valle
Nuevo

PACIFIC OCEAN

NORTH
AMERICA

GUATEMALA

SOUTH
AMERICA

CA 1

Gone Without a Trace

Two journalists hike into the mountains and vanish.

In March 1985, reporter Nick Blake hiked into the misty mountains of Guatemala. With him was Griffith Davis, a photographer from Pennsylvania. The two went in search of a story. They had no idea it would be their last.

For 30 years, the mountains had been home to a mysterious **rebel army**. Government soldiers patrolled the low areas, looking for rebels. The rebels would sneak out to attack the patrols. Then they'd flee into the mountains again.

The rebels avoided reporters. The world knew very little about them. Blake and Davis heard about a wealthy doctor who had left her job to join the rebels. They wanted to tell her story.

Blake and Davis were told to stay out of the mountains. In the past 30 years, tens of thousands of Guatemalans had died. No one could be sure the reporters would come out alive.

But Blake and Davis went anyway. And by April, they had not returned. Their families back in the U.S. had not heard from them, either. On April 8, the men were reported as missing.

A soldier in Guatemala in 1982. Guatemala's civil war lasted from 1960–1996. The violence in Guatemala was at its worst in the early 1980s. Not long after, Nick Blake and Griffith Davis went there to investigate a story.

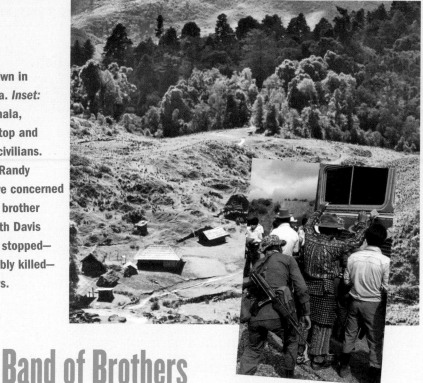

A small town in Guatemala. *Inset:* In Guatemala, soldiers stop and question civilians. Sam and Randy Blake were concerned that their brother and Griffith Davis had been stopped—and possibly killed—by soldiers.

Band of Brothers

A seven-year search finally leads to some answers.

The U.S. government began investigating right away. Officials flew a helicopter over the area where the journalists disappeared. The pilot dropped papers asking for information about the Americans. Weeks passed, then months. The investigation went nowhere.

Nick's brothers, Sam and Randy, decided to search on their own. They took a plane to Guatemala and began to retrace Nick's steps.

The first solid lead came in 1988. The brothers met a schoolteacher in the village of El Llano.

That's where Blake and Davis were last seen alive in March 1985. At the time, El Llano was controlled by **civilian patrols**. Soldiers trained villagers to staff these patrols. Their job was to hunt for rebels. The patrols had a reputation for violence.

The schoolteacher told the Blakes a chilling story. The two journalists were led out of El Llano by civilian patrolmen. They were shot to death outside the village. The patrollers took their clothing, backpacks, cameras, and money. Then they dumped the bodies in the brush and covered them with logs.

Two years later, the Guatemalan military decided to cover up the murder. They ordered a civilian patrol to burn the remains.

For four more years, the Blakes pressed ahead. They wanted the Guatemalan military to admit its role in Nick's murder. But they needed proof.

In early 1992, Sam and Randy Blake made a deal with a man named Felipe Alva. Alva commanded many of the civilian patrols in the El Llano region. He told the Blakes that he knew where to find the two journalists' remains. He would give them to Sam and Randy—for $10,000.

The Blakes agreed to pay Alva. In March

A box containing the remains of a man killed in Guatemala's civil war. Sam and Randy Blake brought two boxes of human remains back to the U.S.

1992, Sam and Randy Blake flew to Guatemala. Alva gave them two boxes of human remains. The Blakes brought the boxes back to the United States.

Did the remains belong to Nick Blake and Griffith Davis? The Blakes turned to a forensic anthropologist to find out.

Douglas Owsley of the Smithsonian Institute examined the contents of the two boxes. He is shown here next to a human skeleton.

The Bone Detective

Can forensic anthropologist Douglas Owsley identify the remains?

On March 27, 1992, two boxes arrived at the office of Douglas Owsley. Owsley is head of physical anthropology at the Smithsonian Institute in Washington, D.C.

Owsley cracked open the two boxes and got to work.

Inside the boxes, the remains lay hidden in a pile of soil. Owsley shook the soil through a screen. The dirt fell through, leaving pieces of bone and metal on the screen.

Owsley found 1,610 bone **fragments**. He could tell right away that he had two sets of bones. One set was white and the other was light yellow. According to Owsley, people have different amounts of body fat and oils in their bodies. When they are burned, their bones turn different colors.

When Douglas Owsley received the remains from Guatemala, he first separated them into 25 plastic bags. These bags were then labeled and x-rayed.

Owsley examined the pieces closely. He found two **occipital bones**. The occipital bone joins the muscles of the neck to the head. Men tend to have larger neck muscles than women. So male occipital bones are also larger. The occipital bones from Guatemala both belonged to men.

On some of the bone fragments, Owsley found thin lines called sutures. Sutures are cracks that separate bones in the skull. Suture lines allow the skull to expand as people grow.

When people reach adulthood, the skull stops growing. The suture lines start to disappear.

Owsley noticed that one skull fragment had a more open suture. It probably belonged to a young man in his 20s. The other fragment had a more closed suture. Owsley guessed that it came from a man in his mid- to late-30s. Blake was 27 when he disappeared. Davis was 38.

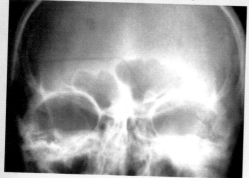

Owsley also discovered two pieces of a **sinus cavity**. The sinus cavity sits in the middle of the forehead about an inch (2.5 cm) above the nose. Owsley fit the two pieces together. He noticed an odd-shaped groove cut into them. An antemortem x-ray of Griffith Davis's sinus cavity showed a similar groove.

Still, Owsley didn't have enough evidence. One piece of the sinus cavity was still missing. He needed it to make a positive identification. And he had no way to prove that the other set of remains belonged to Nick Blake.

SOMETHING STINKS IN TENNESSEE

Death comes to life at the Body Farm.

Ever heard of the Body Farm? The name is a little confusing. It's not a farm. It's a laboratory. And bodies don't grow there. They rot. The Body Farm is a research lab at the University of Tennessee. Douglas Owsley studied there under its founder, Dr. William Bass. Bass started the Body Farm in 1971. It's the only place where forensic experts can study real human bodies as they decay. Students, **FBI** agents, even crime writers study there.

Students at the Body Farm learn to use the human body to solve crimes. They identify **corpses** by their teeth and bones.

Where does the Body Farm get its bodies? Medical examiners often send unclaimed corpses there. Some people even decide to give their body to the lab after they die.

Today, there are almost 400 bodies being studied on the farm.

Owsley was sure that more evidence lay buried in Guatemala. He offered to fly there with the Blakes to help them look.

Back to Guatemala

The Blake brothers return to Guatemala with forensic experts.

On June 11, 1992, Sam and Randy Blake flew back to Guatemala. Owsley went with them. So did another anthropologist named John Verano.

A helicopter dropped members of the team near the murder scene. Led by Felipe Alva, the team hiked to the site of the remains.

Right away, Owsley noticed bone fragments in the soil. He and Verano began carefully digging up the area. They found many pieces of bone, a burned tent stake, and teeth. They even found a pair of wire-rimmed glasses. Sam Blake thought the glasses had belonged to Nick.

Wire-rimmed glasses like these were found near the murder scene. Sam Blake thought they had belonged to his brother Nick.

Making a Match

Owsley makes identifications using the additional materials from Guatemala.

Owsley unpacked the new evidence in his lab. This time, he was sure he had what he needed.

Owsley picked out some teeth and a piece of

DENTISTS OF THE DEAD

Sometimes teeth can solve mysteries.

Forensic odontologists are dentists who study the teeth of the dead. Their work isn't much different from Douglas Owsley's. Often, their job is to identify a person's remains. They do it by comparing the teeth to antemortem dental records and x-rays. They look at the wear on the teeth. They look for signs of decay and dental work. They also study the shape of the teeth and their roots.

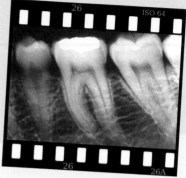

Forensic odontologists compare antemortem dental x-rays like these to postmortem x-rays to help identify victims of accidents and disasters.

Forensic anthropologist Douglas Owsley was able to confirm that the remains belonged to Nick Blake and Griffith Davis.

jawbone. He compared them to x-rays provided by Nick's dentist. Everything matched. The Blakes found a photograph of Nick wearing a pair of wire-rimmed glasses. The glasses perfectly matched the ones found at the site.

Owsley also found the third piece of Griffith Davis's sinus cavity. It fit perfectly with the other two pieces. He compared the completed cavity to an antemortem x-ray of Davis' skull. It matched perfectly.

THE CONCLUSION Owsley was ready to report his findings. The remains recovered in the hills of El Llano belonged to Nick Blake and Griffith Davis.

It had been seven years since the two journalists disappeared. They had finally come home. **24/7**

In this case, an expert identified seven-year-old bones. What can bones reveal about a civilization that's been gone for 4,000 years?

The Princess of
Khok Phanom Di

**An anthropologist uncovers
gravesites that date back more
than 4,000 years. What secrets
will the skeletons reveal?**

Lost Civilization

A long-dead culture is uncovered in Thailand.

Part of the jungle in Thailand is cleared away for buildings and farms. In 1981, when builders cleared land for a new road near the Bang Pakong River, they uncovered ancient bones.

In 1981, Charles Higham heard about an exciting new discovery. Higham teaches anthropology in New Zealand.

The discovery came as builders laid a new road near the Bang Pakong River in Thailand. A bulldozer was carving a path to the top of a hill when it dug up a surprise. Piles of shells appeared in the dirt. Pieces of pottery lay scattered around the hill. These were the remains of an ancient settlement.

Later in 1981, Thai archeologists began excavating, or digging, at the hill. They called the site Khok Phanom Di, "the good mount." Higham decided to visit. When he arrived, he climbed down a bamboo ladder into a small hole. At the bottom, he came face-to-face with the skeletons of prehistoric people.

Higham wanted to know: Who were these people? What was their way of life?

Digging Up the Past

Higham and his team locate stacks of ancient graves.

Higham wasn't able to return to Khok Phanom Di until 1984. In December, he and his

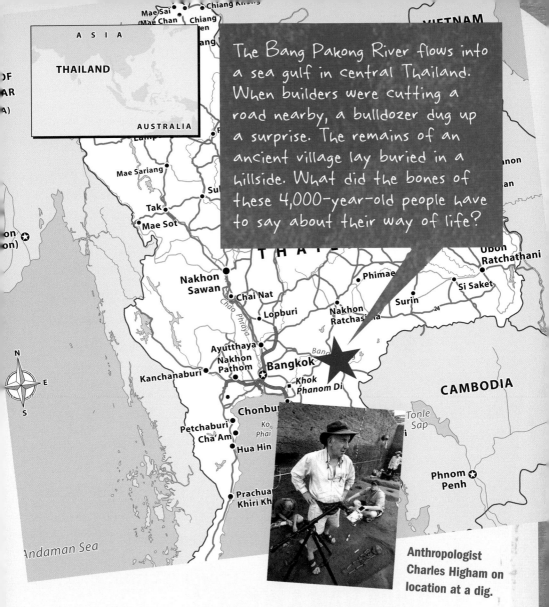

The Bang Pakong River flows into a sea gulf in central Thailand. When builders were cutting a road nearby, a bulldozer dug up a surprise. The remains of an ancient village lay buried in a hillside. What did the bones of these 4,000-year-old people have to say about their way of life?

Anthropologist Charles Higham on location at a dig.

team arrived and started to dig. He worked with a Thai archeologist named Rachanie Thosarat.

For a few weeks, the team dug through heavy dirt. Then the soil began to change. About three feet (.9 m) underground, it grew lighter and more like sand. They continued to dig carefully. Soon the work paid off. A human bone appeared in the soil, then another, and another.

THE EVIDENCE

37

This person was buried with a collection of shell jewelry. These remains were discovered not far from Khok Phanom Di.

The team had found a human grave! And that was just the beginning. Over the next seven months, Higham and his team dug to a depth of 21 feet (6 m). In all, they found 155 graves. The graves lay in rows stacked on top of each other.

Higham then analyzed remains from the lowest graves. The deepest layers in a site are also the oldest. The first grave had been dug around 2000 B.C., he estimated. The people of Khok Phanom Di probably used the cemetery for 500 years.

Through the years, the people had buried their dead in similar ways. Skeletons lay with their heads to the east. Bodies were painted with a red dye. Many of the graves contained shell jewelry and decorated pottery.

Learning from a Princess
The anthropologists find a princess.

After weeks of digging, Higham found an unusual grave. In it were the remains of a wealthy or well-respected woman. She had been buried with jewelry and a headdress made of shells. The grave also held 120,000 shell beads. The beads had probably been sewn onto her clothes. Higham decided to call this woman the Princess of Khok Phanom Di.

Higham knew that the remains belonged to a woman by the shape of the pelvis. Female pelvic bones are generally wider than male pelvises. The added room allows a baby to pass through during childbirth.

Near the grave of the princess lay another grave. It contained the remains of a 15-month-old baby. Higham thinks this infant was the princess's daughter.

The team wondered how the princess won her high position in society. Were her parents rulers? Or was she respected for her own actions? They found the answer in her grave and in her bones. The grave contained a stone used for shaping clay. Next to the stone lay two pebbles used to polish pots.

The princess probably made pottery for a living. Her wrist bones added further proof. The bones had large markings where the muscles attach. The princess had strong wrist and forearm muscles. Chances are she used them to make pots.

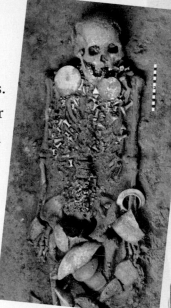

This is the grave of the Princess of Khok Phanom Di. She was buried with jewelry, a headdress, and shell beads—which you can see on her chest.

Charles Higham's team excavating in Thailand. Each year he rents the land from the owner, digs a pit, and fills it in at the end of the field season.

A diagram of a skeleton and the objects with which it was buried. This skeleton was buried with pots, bowls, shell bracelets, shell bangles, and headdress beads. The sketch shows exactly where these objects were found.

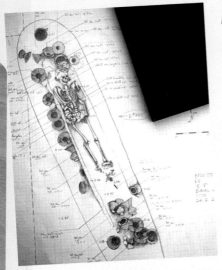

Pottery, then, was important in Khok Phanom Di. The best potters probably lived well. They were wealthy, important people.

A Busy Life

How did the people of Khok Phanom Di make a living?

Higham's team also found plenty of bones from male graves. They gave an important clue to the lifestyle at Khok Phanom Di. Male skeletons tended to be worn down on one side. The wear showed that they probably spent much of their lives paddling canoes.

Khok Phanom Di lies just 14 miles (23 km) up the river from the Gulf of Thailand. About 4,000 years ago, it was even closer to the shore. Men probably paddled to hunt, fish, and trade with other cultures.

Trading was important in Khok Phanom Di. Higham's team studied the princess's beads. They were made from shells that aren't found in central Thailand. Men probably got the shells in a distant town and brought them back by canoe.

Higham's team also figured out the local diet. One body in a grave near the princess had remains of a last meal in its stomach. Scientists found tiny fish bones, fish scales, and rays' teeth. They also found fishhooks at the site.

What Remained

The people of Khok Phanom Di left fascinating clues about their lives.

The Princess was buried next to a male skeleton with no head.

By about 1500 B.C., the village of Khok Phanom Di was empty.

Higham thinks that it became hard for people to find food. There is some evidence that the sea level dropped. The change left Khok Phanom Di farther from the gulf. It became harder to fish and to trade. Eventually, the people simply moved away.

In their graves, they left behind clues to their way of life. They had a wealthy and well-established society. They hunted, fished, and traded with farming communities. They made pottery and created jewelry from coral and shells. Higham learned all that, and more, from studying their **artifacts** and bones. ⏰

THE CONCLUSION

Artifacts are objects made by human beings, usually people who lived long ago.

41

Anthropologist Charles Higham discusses his findings at Khok Phanom Di.

24/7: What were you hoping to learn from your work at Khok Phanom Di?

HIGHAM: We wanted to find the origins of rice farming. We ended up with the opposite — the people there were actually hunters and fishers who interacted with rice farmers moving in from the north.

24/7: What can skeletal remains teach us about an individual?

HIGHAM: A great deal: gender, age, diet, place of origin, health, height, and body mass.

24/7: What can skeletal remains teach us about past cultures?

HIGHAM: They can also teach us a lot about changes in health, demography, human origins, past ways of life, dietary change, origins of agriculture, and disease in the past.

24/7: How are the bones of the "princess" different than those of a modern-day woman?

HIGHAM: She would have been shorter than a modern-day woman. Unless the modern woman was a gymnast, volleyball player, or bricklayer, the princess would have been a lot stronger.

FORENSIC
DOWNLOAD

Here's even more amazing stuff about forensic anthropology for you to dig into.

IN THIS SECTION:

- ▶ the first man to rebuild a HUMAN FACE;
- ▶ why FORENSIC ANTHROPOLOGY has been making headlines;
- ▶ the TOOLS that are used to study bones;
- ▶ whether forensic anthropology might be in YOUR FUTURE!

1849 Boston Doctor Busted!

Dr. John Webster is on trial for the murder of Dr. George Parkman. The evidence? Some false teeth and a part of a human jaw were found near Webster's lab. Parkman's dentist swears that the false teeth and the jaw were Parkman's. The jury believes him. It is the first time in U.S. history that dental evidence puts a murderer in jail.

Key Dates in Forensic

1939 In the Beginning

W. M. Krogman publishes the *Guide to the Identification of Human Skeletal Material*. This marks the beginning of modern **forensic anthropology**.

1957 Bone Stages

Anthropologists Thomas McKern and Thomas Stewart identify the stages a person's bones go through as they grow. This allows anthropologists to look at a skeleton and decide how old the person was when he or she died.

1878 Dwight Makes His Mark

Dr. Thomas Dwight studies human skeletons and writes an essay about them. He is one of the first people to show that human skeletons look different from each other because of gender, age, and race. Dwight is considered the father of American forensic anthropology.

1930s Rebuilding the Face

Michael Gerasimov of the Soviet Union develops a way to rebuild a face on the skull of a human being. He becomes known as the "Man of 1,000 Faces."

Anthropology

How did people figure out that bones could solve mysteries?

1971 Body Farm Opens

Dr. Bill Bass (above), opens the University of Tennessee Anthropology Research Facility (ARF) near Knoxville. It's also called the Body Farm. The lab is a place where anthropologists can study real bodies as they decay. (Some people call the place BARF, for Bass Anthropology Research Facility.)

1984 Anthropology for Human Rights

The Argentine Forensic Anthropology Team is founded. It uses forensic anthropology to recover and identify the remains of people who were victims of human rights abuses around the world.

45

In the News

Forensic anthropology is front-page news.

Anthropologist Builds Faces on Russian Women

MOSCOW, RUSSIA—August 20, 2006

The leading women in Russian history have been dead for hundreds of years. But some of them are about to "show their faces" for the first time.

Many of the wives and mothers of Russia's rulers never posed for paintings. No one knows for sure what they looked like. But their skeletons are preserved in tombs in Moscow, the capital of Russia.

Forensic anthropologist Sergei Nikitin is now collecting their skulls. He plans to rebuild their faces from the size and shape of their bones. He hopes to present images of at least ten of these women in 2007.

Sergei Nikitin from the Moscow Forensic Medical Expertise Bureau has created reconstructions of the faces of Zoe Palaiologina *(left)*, the grandmother of Ivan the Terrible, as well as Elena Glinskaya *(right)*, Ivan's mother.

Forensic anthropologist Kathy Reichs is the real-life inspiration for the TV show *Bones*. She works for medical examiners in North Carolina and in Quebec, Canada. She is a frequent expert witness in criminal trials.

Real Expert Inspires "Bones"

LOS ANGELES—August 30, 2006

Forensic anthropologist Kathy Reichs gets to see her life on TV every week—sort of.

Reichs works for medical examiners in North Carolina and Quebec, Canada. She also teaches anthropology at the University of North Carolina. But she's most famous for writing novels about an anthropologist named Temperance Brennan.

The Fox TV show *Bones* is based on Kathy Reichs's life. But there's a twist. The main character on the show is named Temperance Brennan. She's a forensic anthropologist. And she writes novels about an anthropologist named Kathy Reichs.

On *Bones*, Emily Deschanel plays Dr. Temperance Brennan, a forensic anthropologist. Here, Dr. Brennan looks for clues on a skeleton.

47

The Bare Bones

Have a look at the tools, equipment, diagrams, forms, and other stuff used by a forensic anthropologist.

FORENSIC ANTHROPOLOGISTS' CHECKLIST

When a set of remains needs to be identified, anthropologists know what questions to ask.

1. Are the remains human?
2. Do the remains belong to one person or more than one?
3. What's the PMI?
4. How old was the person when he or she died?
5. What was the person's gender?
6. What was the person's race?
7. What was the person's overall size and weight?
8. Does the skeleton or body show signs of diseases or injuries? Are there any unusual marks that might help identify the remains?
9. What was the manner of death? (There are five choices: natural, accidental, homicide, suicide, or unknown.)
10. What happened to the remains after death? Were they buried? Were they left outside? Were they burned?

PMI stands for postmortem interval. It's the amount of time between death and the time the body was found.

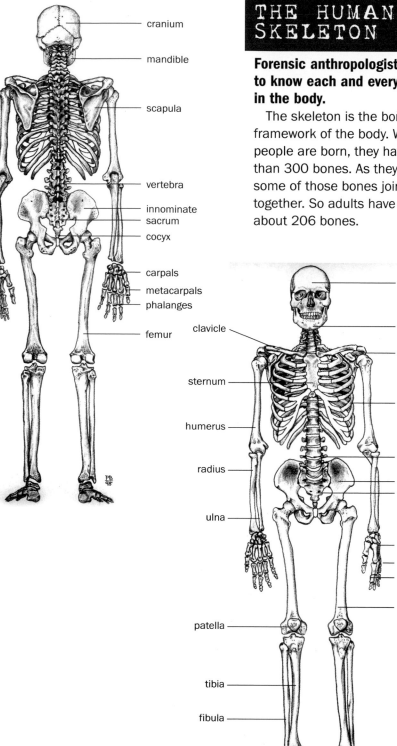

THE HUMAN SKELETON

Forensic anthropologists have to know each and every bone in the body.

The skeleton is the bony framework of the body. When people are born, they have more than 300 bones. As they grow, some of those bones join together. So adults have only about 206 bones.

Labels (left figure): cranium, mandible, scapula, vertebra, innominate, sacrum, cocyx, carpals, metacarpals, phalanges, femur

Labels (right figure): cranium, mandible, scapula, clavicle, sternum, rib, humerus, vertebra, radius, innominate, sacrum, ulna, carpals, metacarpals, phalanges, femur, patella, tibia, fibula, tarsals, metatarsals

49

THE HUMAN HEAD

Forensic anthropologists also have to know the bones of the head.

The cranium is the part of the skull that holds and protects the brain. Eight plate-like bones form the human cranium. They fit together at joints called sutures. The human head also includes 14 facial bones that form the lower front of the skull. They provide the framework for most of the face.

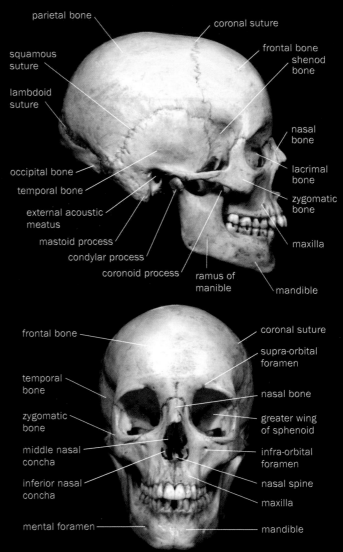

parietal bone · coronal suture · frontal bone · shenod bone · squamous suture · lambdoid suture · nasal bone · lacrimal bone · occipital bone · temporal bone · zygomatic bone · external acoustic meatus · maxilla · mastoid process · condylar process · coronoid process · ramus of manible · mandible

frontal bone · coronal suture · supra-orbital foramen · temporal bone · nasal bone · zygomatic bone · greater wing of sphenoid · middle nasal concha · infra-orbital foramen · inferior nasal concha · nasal spine · maxilla · mental foramen · mandible

[Forensic Quote]
Forensic anthropologist Alison Galloway told whyfiles.org that her job isn't very glamorous. "You spend a lot of time cleaning off yucky bodies," she said. It helps if you "have a strong stomach and an incredibly weak sense of smell."

TOOLS

caliper This measurement tool sizes up smaller bones.

clay, wig, prosthetic eyes Forensic anthropologists use these when they do facial reconstruction on a human skull.

microscope Anthropologists sometimes have to look for details that can't be seen with the naked eye.

FORDISC 3.0 software Anthropologists use this program to help determine the race and sex of a skull. They type in 21 measurements from a skull. The computer does the rest.

TOOLS AND EQUIPMENT

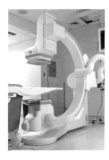

x-ray machine This device uses high-energy beams of light to take pictures of teeth, bones, and organs inside the body.

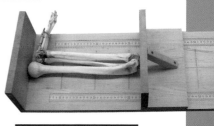

osteometric board This tool is used to find the length of the long bones of a skeleton.

CLOTHING

latex gloves Anthropologists put these on when they handle bone evidence.

Tyvek suit Anthropologists wear these for protection when they work with remains. Tyvek is nearly impossible to tear. It allows only water vapor to pass through. That helps keep **biohazards** away from the body.

HELP WANTED:
Forensic Anthropologist

Is forensic anthropology for you?
Here's a chance to bone up on the field.

24/7: How did you become interested in anthropology?

SLEDZIK: I had always had an interest in biology, history, archaeology, and human evolution. Then I had a really interesting anthropology professor. I was hooked.

24/7: How did you get into the forensic side of anthropology?

SLEDZIK: When I first started (in the 1980s), forensic anthropology was not as popular as it is now. I did a few forensic cases with the college professor I liked. But most of my forensic experience came from the Armed Forces Institute of Pathology. I worked there for 15 years. That's where I learned the techniques and applications of the field.

Paul Sledzik is an anthropologist who works for the National Transportation Safety Board in Washington, D.C. He helped identify victims of the Oklahoma City bombing in 1995, as well as the Flight 93 plane crash on September 11, 2001.

24/7: What type of work do you currently do in forensic anthropology?

SLEDZIK: My current job is a little bit different. Most forensic anthropologists work on individual skeletal cases. I tend to look at disaster situations. I use forensic science in a more comprehensive way. I make sure different agencies work together to identify victims of disasters. I work with family members, federal government officials, and scientists.

24/7: What advice would you give teens who are interested in forensic anthropology?

SLEDZIK: Figure out what they really like about forensic science. Many TV shows portray it in a glamorous way. In reality it's a lot of lab work. You aren't working with criminals. You're working with information and data and samples. So, if it's the glamour that you're after, it may not be for you!

24/7: What part of your job do you enjoy the most?

THE STATS

DAY JOB: Many forensic anthropologists are college professors who teach anthropology. Sometimes they are called by the authorities to help investigations. Anthropologists also work in medical examiner's offices, for the military, or for museums.

MONEY: Anthropology professors can start out making about $30,000 a year. Experienced anthropologists can make more than $100,000 a year.

EDUCATION:
Forensic anthropologists must finish the following:
► 4 years of college
► master's degree in anthropology
► doctorate in anthropology
► practical experience/field work

THE NUMBERS: More than 11,500 individuals from over 100 countries are members of the American Anthropological Association.

SLEDZIK: I enjoy the uniqueness of the job. I like not knowing what will happen day to day. There could be an accident in the next hour that I have to go out to. Or I could get a call from a family member with a unique question. Or there could be a call from a medical examiner with information about a new aspect of victim identification.

Take this totally unscientific quiz to find out if forensic anthropology might be a good career for you.

1 How are you at solving problems?
a) I'm great at finding solutions.
b) Sometimes I have good ideas.
c) You'd better ask someone else.

2 Are you interested in biology and other sciences?
a) I read everything I can find about science.
b) I think it's sort of interesting.
c) I'm only interested in my next meal.

3 How do you react in an emergency?
a) I always stay calm.
b) I usually keep my head.
c) I jump at any noise.

4 Do you get grossed out by bones?
a) Nope. Not that I see them that often, though!
b) I don't mind them.
c) I feel sick just thinking about that question.

5 Are you interested in solving crimes?
a) Yes. I want criminals put in jail.
b) I like to watch crime shows on TV.
c) Someone else can do that.

YOUR SCORE

Give yourself 3 points for every "**a**" you chose.
Give yourself 2 points for every "**b**" you chose.
Give yourself 1 point for every "**c**" you chose.

If you got **13–15 points**, you'd probably be a good forensic anthropologist.

If you got **10–12 points**, you might be a good forensic anthropologist.

If you got **5–9 points**, you might want to look at another career!

HOW TO GET STARTED...NOW!

GET AN EDUCATION
▶ Focus on your science classes, such as earth science and biology.

▶ Start thinking about college. Look for schools with good general anthropology programs.

▶ Read the newspaper. Keep up with what's going on in your community.

▶ Read anything you can find about forensic anthropology. See the books and Web sites in the Resources section on pages 56–58.

▶ Graduate from high school!

NETWORK!
▶ Find out about forensic groups in your area.

▶ See if you can find a local anthropologist who is willing to give you advice.

It's never too early to start working toward your goals.

GET AN INTERNSHIP
▶ Look for an internship with an anthropologist.

▶ Join associations that encourage young people, such as the American Academy of Forensic Sciences Young Forensic Scientists Forum.

LEARN ABOUT OTHER JOBS IN ANTHROPOLOGY
▶ Other employers of anthropologists include medical examiner's offices; the military; federal government agencies; and museums, such as the Smithsonian National Museum of Natural History and the Canadian Museum of Civilization.

Resources

Looking for more information about forensic anthropology? Here are some resources you don't want to miss!

PROFESSIONAL ORGANIZATIONS

American Academy of Forensic Sciences (AAFS)
www.aafs.org
410 North 21st Street
Colorado Springs, CO 80904-2798
PHONE: 719-636-1100
FAX: 719-636-1993

The AAFS provides education for people interested in working in forensics and continuing education for experts already in the field. The organization runs workshops and sessions at its annual meeting that are open to students in middle school and up.

American Anthropological Association (AAA)
www.aaanet.org/index.htm
2200 Wilson Blvd., Suite 600
Arlington, VA 22201
PHONE: 703-528-1902
FAX: 703-528-3546

The AAA was founded in 1902 to promote the science of anthropology, to stimulate and coordinate the efforts of American anthropologists, to foster local and other societies devoted to anthropology, to serve as a bond among American anthropologists and anthropological organizations present and prospective, and to publish and encourage the publication of matter pertaining to anthropology.

American Association of Physical Anthropologists (AAPA)
http://physanth.org/
2200 Wilson Blvd., Suite 600
Arlington, VA 22201
PHONE: 703-528-1902
FAX: 703-528-3546

The AAPA is the world's leading professional organization for physical anthropologists.

American Board of Forensic Anthropology (ABFA)
www.csuchico.edu/anth/ABFA/index.html
California State University, Chico
Chico, CA 95929

The ABFA certifies forensic anthropologists and sets the standards for the field.

Canadian Society of Forensic Sciences (CSFS)
www.csfs.ca
P.O. Box 37040
3332 McCarthy Road
Ottawa, Ontario
Canada K1V 0W0
PHONE: 613-738-0001
FAX: 613-738-1987

The CSFS is a nonprofit professional organization that tries to maintain professional standards and promote the study and enhance the stature of forensic science. Membership in the society is open internationally to professionals with an active interest in the forensic sciences. It is organized into sections representing diverse areas of forensic examination: Anthropology, Medical, Odontology, Biology, Chemistry, Documents, Engineering, and Toxicology.

Centre of Forensic Sciences (CFS)
http://www.mpss.jus.gov.on.ca/english/pub_safety/centre_forensic/about/intro.html
Ministry of Community Safety and Correctional Services
18th Floor
25 Grosvenor Street
Toronto, Ontario
Canada M7A 1Y6

The CFS is one of the most extensive forensic science facilities in North America. The two laboratories conduct scientific investigations in cases involving injury or death in unusual circumstances and in crimes against persons or property.

WEB SITES

The Body Farm
http://www.deathsacre.com/

This site is for the book *Death's Acre*, which is about the creation of the Body Farm at the University of Tennessee.

Forensicanthro.com
http://www.forensicanthro.com/

This Web site is dedicated to providing resources about forensic anthropology.

University of Montana
http://www.anthro.umt.edu/studguid/forensic.htm

This is a Web site for the Department of Anthropology at the University of Montana.

University of Tennessee
http://web.utk.edu/~anthrop/FACbecome.html

This Web site is the University of Tennessee's "Become a Forensic Anthropologist" site.

BOOKS ABOUT FORENSIC ANTHROPOLOGY

Bass, Dr. Bill, and Jon Jefferson. *Death's Acre.* New York: Berkeley Trade, 2004.

Benedict, Jeff. *No Bone Unturned: The Adventures of a Top Smithsonian Forensic Scientist and the Legal Battle for America's Oldest Skeletons.* New York: HarperCollins, 2003.

Hopping, Lorraine Jean. *Bone Detective: The Story of Forensic Anthropologist Diane France.* Washington, D.C.: Joseph Henry Press, 2006.

Joyce, Christopher, and Eric Stover. *Witnesses from the Grave: The Stories Bones Tell.* New York: Ballantine Books, 1992.

Reichs, Kathy. *Déjà Dead.* New York: Pocket Star, 1998.

Ubelaker, Dr. Douglas, and Henry Scammell. *Bones: A Forensic Detective's Casebook.* New York: Edward Burlingame Books, 1992.

BOOKS FOR YOUNG READERS ABOUT FORENSIC SCIENCE

Ferllini, Roxana. *Silent Witness: How Forensic Anthropology Is Used to Solve the World's Toughest Crimes.* Buffalo, N.Y. : Firefly Books, 2003.

Friedlander, Mark P., and Terry M. Phillips. *When Objects Talk: Solving a Crime with Science.* Minneapolis: Lerner Publications, 2001.

Jackson, Donna M. *The Bone Detectives: How Forensic Anthropologists Solve Crimes and Uncover Mysteries of the Dead.* New York: Little, Brown Books for Young Readers, 1996.

Platt, Richard. *Ultimate Guide to Forensic Science.* New York: DK Publishing, 2003.

A

antemortem (an-tee-MORE-tuhm) *adjective* before death

anthropology (an-thruh-POL-uh-gee) *noun* the study of human beings, including their bones, language, and culture

artifact (ar-tuh-FAKT) *noun* an object made by human beings, often many years ago

C

cemetery (sem-uh-TEH-ree) *noun* a place where people are buried after they die

civilian patrol (sih-VIL-yuhn pah-TROLE) *noun* a group of people who are not in the military or the police force but who work to provide order and security

coroner (KOR-uh-nur) *noun* a law officer who oversees the work of the forensic team to find out how people die when the death is sudden or mysterious

corpse (korps) *noun* a dead human body

cranium (KRAY-nee-uhm) *noun* another word for *skull*, especially the part that covers the brain. Plural is *crania*.

D

decomposition (dee-KOHM-puh-ZIH-shun) *noun* the process of decaying, rotting, or breaking down

DMORT (DEE-mort) *noun* a team of experts who help identify victims and prepare them for burial after big disasters or accidents. It stands for *Disaster Mortuary Operational Response Team*.

E

evidence (EV-uh-denss) *noun* materials gathered during an investigation that help solve a crime

excavate (EK-skuh-vate) *verb* to dig up and remove something

expert (ex-PURT) *noun* a person who has knowledge and experience in a certain field. See page 12 for a list of forensic experts.

F

FBI (ef-BEE-eye) *noun* a U.S. government agency that investigates major crimes. It stands for *Federal Bureau of Investigation*.

femur (FEE-mur) *noun* a leg bone in the thigh

forensic anthropologist (fuh-REN-sik an-thruh-POL-uh-jist) *noun* a scientist who studies bones and uses that knowledge in investigations

forensic anthropology (fuh-REN-sik an-thruh-POL-uh-gee) *noun* the study and use of bone knowledge in investigations

forensic odontology (fuh-REN-sik oh-don-TOL-uh-gee) *noun* the science of using teeth and dental records to identify people

forensic pathologist (fuh-REN-sik path-OL-uh-jist) *noun* a medical expert who determines the official cause and manner of death

fragment (FRAG-muhnt) *noun* a part of something that is broken off

G

gender (JEN-dur) *noun* a person or animal's sex, which can be male or female

I

identify (eye-DEN-tuh-fye) *verb* to establish who a person is

L

long bone (long bone) *noun* a bone that has a long shaft and knobs on both ends

M

microscope (MY-kruh-SKOPE) *noun* a tool that makes objects appear larger so they can be studied

O

occipital bone (ok-SIP-uh-tuhl bone) *noun* a bone that sits at the back of the head and joins the muscles of the neck to the head

P

pelvic (PEL-vik) *adjective* describing the pelvic bone, which is a basin-shaped bone below the abdomen

PMI (PEE-em-eye) *noun* the time between when a person dies and when the body is discovered. It's short for *postmortem interval.*

postmortem (pohst-MORE-tuhm) *adjective* after death

R

rebel army (REH-bul AR-mee) *noun* a group of people who act against the government or other authorities

remains (rih-MAYNZ) *noun* the leftover parts of a dead body

S

siding (SYE-ding) *noun* the process of figuring out if a bone is from the left or right side of the body

sinus cavity (SYE-nuss KAV-uh-tee) *noun* a part of the skull located in the middle of the forehead, right above the nose

skeleton (SKEL-uh-tuhn) *noun* the bony framework of the body

skull (skuhl) *noun* the bony frame of the head

sutures (SOO-churz) *noun* cracks that separate the bones in the skull

T

tibia (tih-BEE-uh) *noun* a bone in the shin

tissue (tih-SHOO) *noun* the material in the body that surrounds bones

V

victim (VIK-tuhm) *noun* a person who is injured, killed, or mistreated

X

x-ray (EX-ray) *verb* to photograph a body part with radiation, which allows doctors and scientists to see inside it

Index

Photo Credits: Photographs © 2007: Alamy Images: 51 bottom center left (JG Photography), 32 (Mediscan/Medical-on-Line); AP Images: 30 top (Rodrigo Abd), 44 center (Jim McKnight), 45 top (Paul Sancya), 5 top, 23 (Cliff Schiappa), 34 bottom (Smithsonian), 30 bottom (Linda Spillers); Armed Forces Institute of Pathology: 24, 52; Art Directors and TRIP Photo Library/ Jorge Monaco: 28; Corbis Images: 25 (Yann Arthus-Bertrand), 34 top (Kul Bhatia/zefa), 45 bottom (Diario El Pais/Reuters), 16 (Najlah Feanny-Hicks/SABA), 6 top, 47 top (Will & Deni McIntyre), 51 top (Royalty-Free); DK Images/ Tim Ridley: 5 center, 31; Dr. Charles Higham: 37, 41, 42 (Nigel Chang), 5 bottom, 38, 39 bottom, 39 top, 40; Dr. William C. Rodriguez III: 1 right, 2; Getty Images: 51 top center right (Rob Atkins), 44 top (C Squared Studios), 27, 28 inset (John Hoagland), 48 (Ron Koeberer), cover, 11, 44 bottom (MedioImages), back cover (David Sacks); Lonely Planet Images: 36 (Dennis Johnson), 35 (Chris Mellor); NEWSCOM/Saverkin Alexsander/ Itar-Tass Photos: 6 bottom, 46; Paul Sledzik: 14 bottom, 18, 19, 20, 21, 22; Peter Arnold Inc./ Jim Wark: 15; Peter Brown: 49, 50; Photo Researchers, NY: 10 (Roger Harris), 51 bottom (David Hay Jones/SPL), 4 top, 54 left, 55 (Russell Kightley), 51 top center left (Peter Skinner), 3 (Javier Trueba/Madrid Scientific Films); Phototake/Alain Pol: 14 top; Retna Ltd./Fox Broadcasting Co./Photofest: 47 bottom; Reuters: 45 center (John Sommers II), 4 bottom, 8, 9; Sirchie Fingerprint Laboratories: 1 left, 54 right; Terrie Winson: 51 bottom center right; VEER/ David Robin/Graphistock Photography: 33. Maps by David Lindroth, Inc.

Author's Note

If you Google the term "forensic anthropology," you'll get more than 300,000 results. That's because you aren't the only person out there who's taken an interest in bone detectives! So, read up!

But beware: When reading or writing about real-life stuff, be sure to check your facts. In the process of writing this book, I found that books, Web sites, and articles didn't always agree with each other. One would have a piece of information that I thought was interesting or useful. But, when I compared it to another source, sometimes the information was slightly different.

To be certain something is a fact, use many sources. And, more important, use *trustworthy* sources. Books and articles by the top experts or well-known news writers are a safe bet.

Be careful about trusting the Internet too much. All Internet sites are not created equal, and some aren't even factual! Anyone can post information on the Web. It doesn't mean that it is all well-researched or even true. Check out the Resources section of this book for some of the most helpful sites and books. They'll give you the real lowdown on forensic anthropology.

In researching this book, I had the pleasure of talking with several anthropologists. Each one of them was generous enough to share his experiences with me. After hearing about the cases they work on, I realized just how tough the job of a forensic anthropologist is. They deal with crime, death, and suffering victims all the time. Forensic anthropologists are compassionate people who are truly dedicated to their careers. I hope this book inspires you to think about becoming one.

CONTRIBUTORS:
Charles Higham, anthropologist
Paul Sledzik, forensic anthropologist
Douglas Owsley, forensic anthropologist

ACKNOWLEDGMENTS

I would like to thank the forensic anthropologists who contributed to this book. Their time, effort, and expertise were invaluable to its creation. I would also like to thank Kate Waters, Suzanne Harper, Jennifer Wilson, Elizabeth Ward, and Katie Marsico for their support.

CONTENT ADVISER: Dr. William C. Rodriguez III, Chief Forensic Anthropologist, Armed Forces Institute of Pathology, Washington, D.C.